A Fresh Church School Inspection

Examining the 2023 SIAMS Framework

Margaret James
National Director of SIAMS

GROVE BOOKS LIMITED
RIDLEY HALL RD CAMBRIDGE CB3 9HU

Contents

1 Introduction 3

2 Section 48 Inspection in Church School Education in England ... 6

3 Using a School's Evidence to Make Inspection Judgments 9

4 Potential Unwanted Consequences of Inspection 12

5 Education 'In a Christian Manner' 16

6 Inspection 'In a Christian Manner' 20

7 Conclusion 27

Notes 28

Anglican Association of Directors of Education

First Impression April 2023
ISSN 2041-0964
ISBN 978 1 78827 309 1

1 Introduction

There are approximately 4,700 Anglican and Methodist schools in England. This network consists of schools of a mixture of phases (first, primary, middle, secondary, all-through), statuses (maintained and academy) and designations (voluntary aided, voluntary controlled, foundation, endowed—amongst others). Regardless of context, all can be said to be connected in varying degrees, mainly through diocesan and church structures, by their commitment to enabling the flourishing of pupils and adults. The Church of England Vision for Education, *Deeply Christian, Serving the Common Good,* sums up this commitment and sets out the underpinning theology.[1] It is a bold, aspirational,and theological vision that has a focus on the biblical reference to living 'life in all its fullness.' It is neither dependent upon legislation for its existence and provenance, nor is it criteria-based for the purpose of evaluation and judgment.

It breaks the church's visionary intent down into four main strands. These are educating for:

- Wisdom, knowledge and skills
- Hope and aspiration
- Community and living well together
- Dignity and respect

The four strands provide an accessible structure for the reader, and they encapsulate the overarching vision with their astute and well-chosen terminology. The theological and academic expositions, too, remain both accessible and deep, offering hope for—and about—education in this country. Together, these elements paint a picture of a school system that is inclusive, respectful, dignifying, equitable and contextually responsive. As a result, the Vision offers the possibility of an education that is focused on the flourishing of the individual, which empowers and brings joy, and that is infused with wisdom.

And then we add inspection into the mix, potentially changing the game for us all, and compromising the prospect of the Vision's central theme—life in all its fullness.

The Development of SIAMS

SIAMS is an acronym that is well-known in the church school world. It stands for the Statutory Inspection of Anglican and Methodist Schools and, as the name suggests, it is the means by which all Church of England and Methodist schools in England are inspected. The statutory basis of a SIAMS inspection is set out in law in Section 48 of the 2005 Education Act, that designates the scope of this inspection as follows:

> to report on the quality of the denominational education provided by the school for any pupils to whom denominational education is given by the school…to report on the content of the school's collective worship, and…on the spiritual, moral, social and cultural development of pupils at the school.[2]

Over the last two decades and more, SIAMS has been through a number of different incarnations. Each has systematically built on the previous one/s, refining the criteria against which schools are asked to perform, and against which they are subsequently graded or judged.

Resonance between SIAMS as a means of inspection and what the church actually intends for, and through, the education offered by its schools (its vision) has not always been apparent. However, in the version of SIAMS implemented between April 2018 and July 2023, the connection between the inspection criteria and the Church of England's Vision for Education was explicitly set out through a parity of terminology, with SIAMS making direct use of some of the same wording as the Vision. Examples of this include some of the strand headings, such as 'Strand 2: Wisdom, Knowledge, and Skills'; 'Strand 4: Community and Living Well Together'; and 'Strand 5: Dignity and Respect.' This left the church-school world in no doubt as to the intended connection between inspection and educational vision.

Breaking with the Past

The 2023 SIAMS Framework marks a significant break with the past and with previous approaches to Section 48 inspection. It retains a high bar in terms of accountability, whilst simultaneously introducing a new, context-specific freedom for schools. It does so mainly by asking high-level questions that are focused entirely on impact, rather than by setting out lists of criteria to be met. Schools are invited to share their own stories of how their Christian vision enables pupils and adults to flourish, instead of being expected to jump through pre-ordained generic hoops. This may leave some thinking that the former connection with the Vision for Education has been dispensed with or marginalized, but the links are closer than ever before, and the shared theological provenance deeper.

The term 'theologically rooted Christian vision' appears for the first time in SIAMS 2023. These words are used with the explicit purpose of emphasizing that, to be a truly Christian vision for education, a school's vision requires more than a Bible verse to be added. Instead, it needs to emerge from thought and discussion that finds its roots—its starting place—in biblical and Christian teaching. The idea of school leaders understanding their context and thinking theologically about it is encouraged through the new SIAMS Framework, and is explored in more depth later.

The combination of collaborative inspection methodology, increased consideration of school context, respectful and thorough use of qualitative evidence, explicit coherence between the nature of the evidence and the nature of the judgments, and theologically rooted vision introduces the concept of 'inspecting in a Christian manner.' This is crucial for the church when operating in this particular area of education.

Connected to this, and important to note, are the potentially unwanted consequences of inspections and of the power imbalance that they tend to create. These consequences on school leaders are numerous and they are likely to be negative, if not taken into account by those who have the power to mitigate them.

The 2023 SIAMS Framework is explicitly rooted in—and reliant upon—robust qualitative evidence. This is not new, as the legal scope of SIAMS has not changed since 1992. However, the evidence is expressed ultimately through judgments rather than by grades, introducing greater coherence between evidence and outcomes. It does so without changing the everyday agenda for schools, without breaking the inspection connection with the 2016 Church of England Vision for Education, and without lowering the bar in terms of standards. In fact, it is an approach to church school inspection that is both radically different from, and radically the same as, its recent predecessors. It is radically different in its explicit embrace of qualitative evidence and contextually appropriate judgment-making, and radically the same inasmuch as it does not reimagine what it means to be a church school.

2 Section 48 Inspection in Church School Education in England

The Church of England has been a significant partner in the provision of state-funded education in England since 1811, when Joshua Watson established the National Society for Promoting the Education of the Poor in the Principles of the Established Church throughout England and Wales. Fifty years later, in 1861, there were around 12,000 free-to-attend schools for local communities, operating in union with the National Society—a number that, in 2023, whilst far lower, is still educating around one million pupils. By any standards, this was—and remains—a phenomenal achievement, demonstrating Watson's original belief that 'the way out of poverty and ignorance was education, not only to train people in basic skills but also to build character.'[3] His vision and intent live on today in church school education.

Reflecting the Teachings of Christ

A church school, Christian-vision-driven education should, at least, reflect the teaching of Jesus to, for example, love one another (John 13.34–35); to care for those in society who might otherwise be neglected (Luke 10.25–37); to forgive (Matt 6. 15); and to offer all who stumble and make mistakes the opportunity of redemption (Rom 5.6–15). It is an approach to education that is rooted in the biblical aspiration to live life as fully as possible (John 10.10), flourishing as unique individuals made in the image of God (Gen 1.27).

This is summed up by Worsley:

> Whenever we dream about the ideal school, it is not only a place of forgiveness but one of redemption. It is a place where those who are broken are made whole, where *shalom* is brought into being and where healthy development is allowed to develop. It is where the whole child matters and where every child matters, a place where the curriculum is balanced to the needs of the area and the range of children, where the school's systems reflect the kingdom of God in bringing about redemption. So let us imagine a school where love is explicit, where forgiveness operates, where work is balanced with adequate rest and play.[4]

However, to become a real, life-changing experience for those who attend a church school, this needs to move beyond aspiration to be lived out in and by each church school community, with a clear vision that shapes and drives their work.

In many ways, a church school education is a countercultural educational offer, made by schools that remain subject to all the demands and accountability measures to which all other schools are also subject. Ofsted inspection expectations are the same; DfE accountability is the same; and local authority, diocesan or multi-academy trust scrutiny is the same. But the vision comes from a different place, deeply rooted as it is in the Christian faith.

The Requirement for SIAMS Inspections

For church schools, there is then an additional regime of accountability—SIAMS. Understandably, this has a mixed reception in and amongst the diverse range of schools that are subject to it. Some seem to welcome SIAMS with open arms; and yet it is, at times, possible to hear a collective inspection-opposed groan across the country.

The additional inspection of church schools is not actually the idea (or fault!) of the church itself. In 1992, Section 48 of the Education Act introduced for the first time the legal requirement for the inspection of certain aspects of the work of schools that have a designated religious character.[5] Successive education acts have since retained and further clarified the detail and scope of this legal obligation, thus establishing the basis for the system that is referred to today as 'SIAMS.'

SIAMS has brought to the fore matters of spirituality and spiritual development

In various iterations from 2005 onwards, the church's national Section 48 inspection requirements have variably emphasized, amongst other foci, Christian distinctiveness, effectiveness, Christian values and Christian vision. SIAMS has brought to the fore matters of spirituality and spiritual development; leaders' monitoring and evaluation of aspects of schools that are specifically related to their Anglican and / or Methodist foundation; and the provision and impact of church school priorities. It has also led to the embedding of influential terms such as 'courageous advocacy,' 'agents of change' and 'excellence' into common church school parlance.

It is fair to say that, over time, these emphases within SIAMS have led to general and widespread improvements in many aspects of what it means to be a church school. Often driven by the desire to be awarded the highest possible grades, schools and diocesan / Methodist education teams have worked together to understand, address, and exemplify the various criteria within whichever version of Section 48 (SIAS or SIAMS) was in place. As a result, over time (albeit, I suggest, unintentionally) many aspects of a performance culture have become embedded as driving forces within SIAMS and, by extension, within church schools themselves. However, this has occurred with little or no examination of the theoretical basis and real-life implications of such a culture. More of this in chapter four.

What it Means to Inspect a Church School

Since the 2010 Academies Act and the establishment of an increasingly competitive and market-driven culture within education, the challenge for the church to have, and to communicate, a clarity of foundation, vision and purpose for its involvement in the sector has become more pressing.[6] As Astley explains:

> It is too easy in some contexts to forget the difference that Christianity should make to education, and to smooth out the radical disjunction between the wisdom of the cross and the wisdom of the world. But Jesus proclaimed first and foremost a good news for the poor. Whatever else we claim to do 'in his name,' we must share *this* mission.[7]

The Church of England faces this challenge head on through its Vision for Education; but therein lies an additional task—that is, to ensure coherence and integrity between the Vision and its own system of accountability through SIAMS. This is a difficult challenge, given the often punitive and terrorizing discourse that surrounds school inspection in England.

The most important considerations underpinning the changes to SIAMS from September 2023 are an extensive coherence rooted in integrity, and a commitment to school inspection being conducted 'in a Christian manner.' For SIAMS to be Christian in manner, and for it to be fully coherent and characterized by systemic integrity, there should be a single logic throughout. This should begin in the fundamental basis of the inspection, extend through the questions that require an answer (the evidence), be woven into the methodology and, ultimately, be evident in the way in which the outcomes are expressed (the judgments). Any break in this thread would automatically introduce a disjunction and create dissonance.

Within the 2023 SIAMS Framework, scrutiny of impact remains rigorous; extensive and probing questioning remains central; a broad and robust evidence-base remains key; formative school improvement remains an important aim; and a coherent systemic integrity permeates. Within SIAMS, all of this is framed by a theologically-rooted Christian vision.

3 Using a School's Evidence to Make Inspection Judgments

Church-school leaders are likely to be familiar with SIAMS inspection lines of enquiry that address issues such as spirituality, relationships, worship, the impact of Christian vision and so forth. They will have been invited to tell their stories of what life in the school is like, and of the impact they believe the Christian-vision-driven work is having. Parents will have been invited to share their views and experiences, as will children and other school partners. This is a crucial element of a SIAMS inspection—storytelling. Time for the school community to actually tell stories of their lived experience; for leaders to explain the why, what and how of the work of the school; and for all to share how they believe the Christian vision is making a difference to lives.

Narrative Evidence

It is unlikely that most SIAMS-related areas of the work of the school can be captured by quantitative numerical evidence or data. On the contrary, by its very nature, SIAMS heavily relies on evidence that is largely narrative. This type of evidence is relevant within SIAMS because of the basic scope, or content, of Section 48 inspection, as set out in law. A SIAMS inspector is tasked, legally, with inspecting the school's worship life; the quality of religious education; and pupils' spiritual, moral, social and cultural development. Therefore, the vast majority of the evidence will be indisputably qualitative in nature.

The evidence gathering itself will, variably, take the form of inspection conversations, document scrutiny, observations of normal events and interactions, alongside triangulation—or checking out the validity of evidence across a range of different sources. If the school is an academy, leaders of the trust will be involved as a matter of priority; and the views of representatives of the diocesan board of education or Methodist Academies and Schools Trust, alongside local church/es with which the school has partnerships, will be sought.

The inspector needs to answer the Inspection Questions, and they need to have enough evidence to support their conclusions.[8] They will, therefore, be highly reliant on school leaders to provide as much evidence as they have. For example, Inspection Question 3 asks how collective worship is enabling pupils and adults to flourish spiritually. To be satisfied, the inspector would need to understand, for example:

- What the school understands by spiritual flourishing.
- How they provide an environment within which this is possible.
- Which partners help with this area of the school's work, and what difference they make.
- How school leaders know that pupils and adults are flourishing spiritually.

The inspector will not work through a set list of generic criteria or questions to gather this evidence, and they will not have preconceived expectations related to provision and methodology. Rather, they will ask the school to explain, to illustrate and to provide their evidence. For example:

- If the school actually has no prayer life, how can they claim or demonstrate that this is enhancing spiritual flourishing?
- If pupils are no more than passive observers of worship, how can it be possible that this is enabling them to grow spiritually?
- If adults do not attend worship, in what ways are they being enabled to flourish spiritually as part of the school community?
- And how do leaders *know* whether and how pupils and adults are flourishing spiritually?

Making a Judgment

From September 2023, the SIAMS-generated knowledge about a school that is gathered through the Inspection Questions is being summed up and expressed as a *judgment*. This marks a change in inspection practice, moving as it does, for the first time, away from awarding a grade that is subsequently translated to a number (1, 2, 3, 4). It is thus a radically different approach to reporting inspection outcomes.

It can be wrongly assumed that to inspect equates to, or by definition necessitates, awarding grades. This is not the case. Successful and rigorous fulfilment of the remit of inspection does not require a grading system, despite grades (usually on a four-point scale) having become practically synonymous with school inspection over the years.

Taking qualitative evidence that is, by nature, open to interpretation and treating it as if it were objective, attributing to it a grade that some may describe as arbitrary is, at best, rather misleading. Expressing it instead as a judgment honours the nature of the evidence, as well as enabling the inspection to make a valuable formative contribution to the school's ongoing improvement.

There are only two broad judgments in the 2023 SIAMS Framework—J1 and J2.

- J1: Through its vision and practice, the school is living up to its foundation as a church school and is enabling pupils and adults to flourish.
- J2: The school's vision and practice are not enabling it to fully live up to its foundation as a church school.

It is often wrongly assumed that a choice between two judgments is only appropriate for quantitative data, or that they are a quantitative expression of data—which is also incorrect. Judgments such as these can be used to good effect when expressing nuanced, multi-faceted, complex, often qualitative evidence that is open to interpretation. Consider, for example, similarities with the criminal justice system. Juries hear evidence from a range of sources, of a variety of types, and with varying degrees of plausibility. They consider it, discuss their interpretations, seek coherence across the whole, and ultimately arrive at their judgment—a verdict. That verdict is expressed as guilty or not guilty. The evidence was not straightforward; it was not necessarily clear-cut; it was open to interpretation; and the final judgment is coherent with that.

The new judgments in SIAMS provide a formative snapshot, indicating the effectiveness of the school's theologically-rooted, Christian-vision-driven work. They also highlight on which areas of school life leaders need to focus in order to improve, or to keep improving. If the inspector has sufficient evidence to answer each inspection question positively, they will award J1. It is likely, however, that for many schools there will be at least one inspection question in which there is not enough evidence. In this case, the inspector will award J2, and they will use the J2 criteria to highlight which areas require more work and evidence.

Each J2 criterion refers directly back to an Inspection Question, focusing leaders' attention onto their next steps. Yet the judgments neither condemn, nor arbitrarily and superficially claim to quantify, that which is not easily measured (that is, qualitative evidence). They are judgments that are coherent with the type of evidence that has been collected, and they highlight in a formative manner where steps to improvement can be made, for the benefit of the school community as a matter of urgent priority.

4 Potential Unwanted Consequences of Inspection

In theory, inspection of any type can turn an area of work into one that is disproportionately shaped by the prospect of punitive accountability and a potentially destructive power imbalance. This notion may be all too familiar to those on the ground, who have been subject to inspection at any time during their career and who have felt the weight of an inspector's power over them.

As a result, inspection has the ability to create a culture in which 'value displaces values,' and in which compliance becomes a key feature.[9] If true, this can potentially (and inadvertently) create an overriding culture in schools in which people focus their energy and attention onto gaming the system in order to be successful, instead of enabling real flourishing, based on the context and genuine need of individuals. Research with church school headteachers and governors suggests that this theoretical possibility is, in fact, an everyday reality for some.[10]

The church has both a moral and a theological responsibility to consider these potential unwanted consequences when taking, and enacting, its place in the field of school inspection.

'Stage Management'

One such consequence, in which people knowingly engage, is gaming the system and taking part in window dressing.[11] One obvious reason for this is the perceived need to ensure that the image of the school presented to the inspector is of such quality, compliance and acceptability as to secure a positive inspection outcome.

It is important to acknowledge the difference between a school community collating and presenting an image of itself that is representative of everyday practice yet condensed into the day of inspection, and a school community materially altering the fabric of the 'stage' for the purpose of inspection.[12] Such alterations might be made to the school's physical appearance, documentation and classroom practice, in order to present an image that aligns with the inspection criteria. Examples might include making sure that children can recite rehearsed definitions of the Trinity, or putting up new displays or Christian symbols just before the day of the inspection. There is no significant sense of criticism here; simply an observation that this is one of the ways in which our human nature tends automatically to act to preserve and protect our sense of self, particularly within a regime of accountability such as inspection.

Unintended Consequences

As well as intentional stage management by school leaders in a conscious attempt to influence the outcome of an inspection, there are other unintentional consequences:

- The prospect of inspection can cause school leaders to experience something of a sense of tunnel vision in which they, possibly unknowingly, put a disproportionate focus on the elements of school life and performance that an inspector will examine, rather than on those that they themselves value. Lists of inspection criteria can have this effect, encouraging (or forcing) school leaders to tick certain boxes in order to secure a successful outcome.
- There can also be a preoccupation with ensuring that all inspection paperwork and documentation are completed and kept up to date, *just for the purposes of inspection*, despite the burden that this puts onto school leaders. Within the education culture in England, with its prevalence of inspection and accountability, adherence to rules and expectations related to paperwork is particularly noteworthy—whereas the extent to which it all contributes to the real life of the school is questionable.
- Whilst it is obvious to those involved in school leadership that schools in different contexts have different needs, one of the unintended consequences of school inspection is the narrowing of the types of provision only to those deemed acceptable to those who have the power to make judgments. This can remove the nuanced, contextual appropriateness of a school's work, as well as hamper leaders' ability to meet some of the real-life needs that may be right before them.

These intended and unintended consequences have been taken into account in the writing of the 2023 SIAMS Framework. This is important because, if left unaddressed, they can have the effect of creating a performance paradox in schools, in which performance in areas that are measured through inspection might improve (according to the criteria used for judgment), whilst what some might call 'actual' performance might not.[13]

It appears that school inspection can have all of these consequences regardless of whether the inspection is regarded as being high or low stakes. SIAMS inspection can be described as being relatively low stakes compared with the high stakes of Ofsted, since its specific legal remit prevents it from straying into outcomes that may become related to job/leadership retention and/or directive academy conversion. Yet research suggests church school leaders might in reality (albeit involuntarily or unknowingly) succumb to such inspection-driven behaviours in order to comply with the criteria of a powerful inspection system, tick certain boxes and receive a favourable outcome, even when the stakes are deemed to be relatively low.[14]

Power at Play in Inspection

Within school inspection in its current and predominant format there are two main actors. On the one hand is the inspector—the expert in terms of their knowledge and experience; the one with the ability to make judgments that are lasting in their influence on the opinions of others. On the other hand is the school leader whose work is being inspected. This leader—arguably the expert in the life of their school, yet traditionally subject to the power of the inspector—is, in many ways, regarded as being at the mercy of the decisions and judgments that will be made.

The inspector's power emerges from a combination of their position, their knowledge, their experience and their expertise. Over time and reinforced by the structure of the education inspection system, this has led to power being routinely exercised by one professional over another or over a group. Consequently, we have seen the creation of a power imbalance that has become virtually synonymous with school inspection.

Almost imperceptibly, many school leaders have culturally assimilated the current education system that is heavily shaped by the performative requirements of inspection, and by the contingent power play. As a result, leaders often accept this culture and possibly barely recognize that another different normal could exist. They may even find that they welcome it, due to the certainty, or the command and control structure, that such specific direction creates.

The power at work in school inspection relies upon compliance to be effectively exercised

It is also interesting to note that the power at work in school inspection relies upon the compliance of all involved for its ability to be effectively exercised. In-school professionals involved in this outworking of power may be hardly aware of its existence, and even less cognisant of their own complicity in the foothold that it gains. The power extends its influence through what can be described as net-like structures, each person playing their part in ensuring that it becomes established and embedded within acceptable and routine organizational structures and protocols.

This is not necessarily as negative as it might first sound. Within education, it can bring about empowerment for people and it can therefore be difficult to argue against—for example, when seen as a means of accountability that results in school leaders focusing on the needs of the most vulnerable in their communities.

There is nothing straightforward about power and it is certainly not easily removed from any regime of accountability. However, awareness of its existence and of its potential consequences is an important aspect of the way in which the church fulfils its responsibilities in the field of school inspection.

In the 2023 SIAMS Framework, the imbalance of power has been somewhat mitigated by the increased emphasis on the expertise and contextual knowledge of school leaders. Without diminishing the authority and expertise of the inspector, the profile of leaders' expertise in their own school's context has been raised. By honouring these two equally important components of inspection—inspector expertise and school leader expertise—the new SIAMS Framework rebalances the power that is at play, with the aim of ensuring fairness, accuracy, robustness and a new depth of dignity and integrity within the process of school inspection.

5 Education 'In a Christian Manner'

Church of England Education

It is reasonable to assume that any system of school *inspection* should be resonant with the system of *education* on which it is making judgments. Anything else is likely to lead to disconnection and disjuncture between the two, resulting in arguably frustrating accountability processes and unhelpful outcomes.

The Church of England Vision for Education acts as a touchstone in Anglican church-school education, a point of reference and a source of inspiration, giving a sense of meaning and purpose to work that can, at times, appear to be multi-faceted and complex. It keeps everyone focused on the reason for the work they are doing, putting theological thinking front and centre. It also provides a framework for judging the validity, or the rightness, of policy-making, decisions and actions. In other words, it is both a strategic and an operational filter for the work of the Church of England in education.

The four strands of this vision have harmony with the education in a Christian manner that is expounded by Astley and which he describes as being 'characteristic of Christianity rather than distinctively Christian.'[15]

As a basic premise, he argues that any education put forward as being Christian in nature must:

> be congruent with the ends of Christianity, with the end that *is* Christ... But to qualify as Christian education it must retain some contact with its centre. The enterprise, in its furthest reaches, must somewhere bear the imprint of *his* touch, something of the whorls and configurations of his mark.

One of the ways in which a church school education does this is by valuing each person simply for who they are and the gifts they have. It ascribes to them dignity, made as they are in the image of God, and it does all it can to enable them to flourish holistically. It is a countercultural, Christlike form of education that can be described as education as *praxis*—the moral imperative that regards the education of both self and other as a worthy and far-reaching endeavour.

Theologically rooted Christian Vision

A theologically rooted education such as that described by Astley, set out within the Church of England Vision for Education, and reflected in the 2023 SIAMS Framework, needs to be firmly grounded in each school's understanding of its own mission and purpose—in other words, in its own theologically-rooted Christian vision. Unless personalized, this form of education remains an academic aspiration at best and a vague pie-in-the-sky idea at worst. No school leader has time or energy to expend on such activity.

Yet the prospect of rooting the work of a school in theology should not be the straw that breaks the camel's back. Each Anglican or Methodist school was originally set up with the legal remit of providing, to those in the local community who were and are most in need, an education that resonates with its Christian foundation. This is a legal requirement for church schools; it is expressed in their foundation or trust deed and it continues to this day. A twenty-first-century way of expressing this legal foundation is through a school's theologically rooted Christian vision.

In thinking this through it is important to realize that, despite some arguments to the contrary, there is no such thing as a neutral education. Every education, indeed every person, is rooted in, and views the world from, one perspective or another. Because of the reality of this positionality, it is untrue to say that schools that are not church schools—community schools—offer a neutral education. This would suggest that community schools are occupying the hypothetical moral high ground of supposed neutrality, whilst their church-school counterparts are doing the opposite—a notion that skews the reality of the situation.

The Church of England makes no ill-founded claims of neutrality and it does not conceal the basis of its educational offer. On the contrary, through its vision it explains it clearly and sets it out for all to see. Moreover, in a deeply Christian way, it offers its schools freely to local communities for the common good, welcoming people of all backgrounds, faiths, cultures and beliefs. Church schools invite the local community in; they accept people as being made in the image of God; and they seek to enable each one to flourish by developing their gifts and talents. They do this for the theological reasons contained within the four strands of the Church of England's Vision for Education.

A church school's theologically rooted Christian vision builds on this overarching aim. Its vision will be rooted in an understanding of what the community needs (its context) and in what the Christian faith teaches about that need:

- Does the community most need hope? If so, what does Christianity say to us about being hopeful?

- Are families crying out for aspiration? Where does the Bible speak of this?
- Do people need, more than anything, to learn respectful and dignifying generosity? If this is a pressing need, what can we learn from Christian teaching about this?
- Is there an urgent need in the community for a place of refuge and safety above all else? What is Christ's example here?

The list of possible community needs goes on, with many requiring all of the above and more. But what are the most pressing and characterizing needs of an individual school community? Discerning this and reflecting on it theologically, as briefly outlined, is key to the creation of a contextually appropriate, theologically rooted Christian vision.

What a church school education does *not* do is impose or expect Christian belief. It does not discriminate against those who do not profess a Christian faith. It does not have a hidden ulterior motive. Instead, it is an educational offer that is unashamedly rooted in God's love for all of humanity. Without understanding the school's legal basis as a church school, the needs of the community and what Christian love can look like in action, it is not really possible to have a theologically-rooted Christian vision. But when the school's legal basis as a church school is clearly understood, alongside the needs of the community and the reality of what Christian love can look like in action, this provides the framework for creating a school's theologically-rooted Christian vision.

It really is no more complicated than this.

Such a vision may be expressed in, or accompanied by, a Bible verse—but it may not. It may be related to a parable—but it may not. It will always, however, reflect the needs of the community, be an expression of Christ's love for all people, and find its original roots in the teaching of the Bible and of the Christian faith.

St Mark's Junior School is in an unusual position. It is a Voluntary Aided church school, whereas its feeder infant school is a community school. That means that many of the children entering the school come from families who did not specifically choose a church school education.

In 2019, its new head teacher undertook a major consultation exercise on the school's vision and values. The challenging aspect of this was the discomfort of a significant minority of the school community with the use of the word 'God' in the vision. As servants of the whole school community, the governors decided that it would be wrong to create unease by insisting on using the word 'God' in this way.

Their vision statement is: *Growing Together, Becoming All We Are Created To Be*. This vision is theologically rooted in the notion that as a church school, it is a community where everyone matters because everyone bears the image of God as created beings. Furthermore, drawing on St Paul's teaching on the interdependence of God's community in 1 Corinthians, the school grounded its vision in the importance of everyone working together to support each other's flourishing. This vision is expressed through four values:

- *F*orgiveness
- *A*spiration
- *C*ompassion
- *E*ngagement

These values form the FACE of St Mark's. Each value is earthed in a story from the life of Jesus that enables children to understand its meaning and significance. The vision and values are continuously referenced in all aspects of school life and drive all key decisions, from choice of curriculum content to the way in which finances are deployed. They offer a truly Christian understanding of what *becoming all we are created to be* means.

St Mark's seeks to be *deeply Christian* by focusing on its role as the parish school. The church, although not physically close, is spiritually close through joint partnership in a wide range of activities through the year which deeply enrich school life, including services at key points in the church year. The school is therefore integral to the church's ministry in the wider parish. In this way it is *serving the common good*. This came to the fore when the church played a key role in supporting the school community through a pupil bereavement.

God may not be mentioned in the vision statement but is experienced through, and named in, the everyday life of the school.

In November 2022 (and thus according to the 2018–2023 SIAMS schedule), St Mark's was judged as excellent in all three aspects of its SIAMS inspection.[16]

6 Inspection 'In a Christian Manner'

As already outlined, the scope of a Section 48 inspection is set out by law, not by the church, and it relates to religious education, collective worship and spiritual, moral, social and cultural education. However, the *manner* in which this inspection is conducted is entirely within the remit of the church to establish, encourage, evaluate and ensure.

According to Astley's understanding of 'in a Christian manner,' SIAMS inspection must bear the imprint of the touch of Christ. It would be foolish to interpret this as being uncritical, indulgent or fluffy. Compassion and fairness are not the same as unquestioning acceptance, blind agreement or unfounded, undeserved affirmation, regardless of effectiveness. The example set for us by Christ himself could not be further from this, rooted as it is in speaking truth to power and courageous advocacy for our neighbours. Understanding this is central to understanding what inspection in a Christian manner may look like in practice.

Contextual Evidence

Unsurprisingly, SIAMS is an evidence-led process. Inspection Questions must be answered with responses that are evidence-based. However, it is important to understand that evidence comes in many shapes and sizes. Furthermore, it must always be coherent with the purpose for which it is required and with the nature of the specific context.

Quantitative evidence has its place in SIAMS, for example, in relation to numbers of students studying GCSE or A-level RE and their subsequent grades. However, it is the predominance of *qualitative* evidence that is most essential to accurate and fair SIAMS judgments, yet this evidence is not as objective and clear-cut as some may like to think.

It is important for a SIAMS inspector to understand what it is like to be part of a particular church school community—what the reality is. For example:

- Are people treated well?
- Do they feel that they belong and are valued and accepted as being made in the image of God?
- Are people shown how to be kind to others?

- Are they empowered to question, challenge, be curious, become a leader or an advocate for others?
- And, crucially, what examples, stories or anecdotes can they share that exemplify this and that give weight to their feelings and lived experience?

Collation of this type of evidence is central to an inspector being able to then use their expertise, evaluate with rigour and make an accurate judgment on whether a school's Christian vision is having the intended impact or not—whether it is making a real difference to people's lives. Their judgment-making subsequently incorporates reference to people's accounts of their experiences, and to their stories of impact—this is qualitative narrative evidence.

Such narrative evidence may look very different, depending on context, from one school to another, being both nuanced and complex to deal with. Yet grappling with it and making sense of what it means in context for the people concerned is one of the aspects of a SIAMS inspection that arguably sets it apart from other inspectorates, and it is definitely worth the effort. SIAMS honours the lived experience of people by means of this evidence, accepting that context can make all the difference to both process and outcomes.

Welcoming such qualitative evidence and being open-minded, whilst retaining focus and clarity, are key features of inspecting in a Christian manner. It is an approach that allows appropriate individuality to take precedence over generic and potentially arbitrary expectations, yet without sacrificing quality and high standards in the process.

Discursive Yet Focused

Key to a successful inspection are the inspector's lines of enquiry. The inspector will have arrived at these after careful consideration and evaluation of all pre-inspection-day evidence, such as document and website scrutiny, discussions with the head teacher and examination of any publicly available information about the work of the school. Where there appear to be notable gaps in evidence or significant questions, a carefully worded line of enquiry provides school and inspector with a pathway to enable them, together, to fill the gap or answer the question. Lines of enquiry, in short, enable the gathering of relevant evidence so that the inspector can analyze and evaluate in depth, thereby making fair and accurate judgments in the limited time available.

In inspection, as in life more generally, one of the best ways to find out something is to talk with a person who is both knowledgeable and who feels at ease. When people are at ease, they tend to open up and speak fluently, which enables the other person to understand. The best way for a SIAMS inspector to get under the skin of a school, to understand what impact its work is really having, is to have honest and open *conversations* with the people who are, arguably, the experts—those in the school community. It is not to fire endless lists of generic questions at them; not to assume possession of knowledge that is not yet possible; not to maximize people's feelings of nervousness and stress; not to presuppose outcomes—but to discuss and to listen. The discursive conversations will be shaped by the inspector's lines of enquiry; their probing, focused and, at times, challenging questions; and their knowledge of inspection. But they will also be shaped by the knowledge and expertise that is held within the school.

The inspection conversations may appear to be meandering at times, but they should always be centred on enabling the inspector to gather the relevant evidence that will allow them to make fair and accurate judgments. It is a logical and coherent juxtaposition.

An inspector who is inspecting in a Christian manner will carry out their work with a laser focus, but one that allows for an unexpected change of direction if so led by the evidence. Such an inspector will have clarity over what questions they need to be able to answer by the end of the day, and they will have an idea of what type of evidence may enable them to do this.

Inspecting in a Christian manner allows for a change of direction if so led by the evidence

However, there is a difference between an inspector being aware of the type of evidence that they *may* see, and being blinded by an intransigent preconception of what they *expect* to see. Inspectors, as with all people with all tasks, approach inspection from a certain position—their own. Positionality is a reality of being human, and it should not be shied away from or denied for fear of appearing to lack objectivity and thus authority. Rather, it is awareness of one's positionality that has the potential to illuminate reality and to move a person from where they stand and look, to where another stands and looks. I can argue endlessly that I am looking at a 6. But it is only when I move to stand next to you that I realize that from where you stand it is, in fact, a 9. Intransigence is rarely a helpful quality in achieving shared clarity and understanding.

So, in the context of a SIAMS inspection, an inspector may have seen many times before, for example, a well-trodden path to the creation of a spiritually flourishing school community. Therefore, they may arrive at a school with some clarity over what evidence they might expect to gather. However, *because of its context* and whilst remaining faithful to its foundation as a church school, this particular school may work very differently from the ten schools previously visited by the inspector. It may use different resources, implement different strategies, communicate through different media, follow different pathways of Christian worship and spiritual nourishment. This reality requires the inspector to set aside any preconceptions related to provision, to be open-minded and to focus predominantly on outcomes. Are pupils and adults in this church school community flourishing spiritually? That is the question that must be answered, with clarity of understanding of what is sought but with an open-minded approach as to how it might be achieved.

Authoritative and Expert Yet Collaborative

All this talk, of perspective, positionality, inspection conversations and evidence that is open to interpretation, may lead some to conclude that a SIAMS inspector either relinquishes their authority and expertise, or that they have very little in the first place. This could not be further from the truth.

Whilst it is reasonable and respectful to acknowledge that the school leaders are experts in the life of the school and that the inspector is not, it is also important to recognize that the inspector is the expert in inspecting and that the school leaders are not. This means that the inspector is best placed to gather, analyze and evaluate targeted, relevant evidence, using it to make accurate and fair judgments. Given the nuance and complexity of dealing with a largely qualitative evidence base, this is not for the faint-hearted.

When left unquestioned, an inspector's authority and expertise can be deemed automatically to come hand in hand with power—power that can, as discussed earlier, be punitive in nature. Whilst not possible to fully remove an imbalance of power from inspection, it is possible to mitigate it and to introduce an appropriate balance. This comes through understanding the respective areas of expertise of both inspector and school leaders, by knowing when and how they should draw on each other. It is an approach that is rooted in remembering that, as the church in education, we act as the body of Christ. Each person has a part to play and the flourishing success of the whole body relies on each one not only playing their own part, but on them also valuing and respecting the role played by others. We need each other; we each bring something valuable to the whole; and, when enacted with respect, the inspector's authority and expertise can lead to meaningful collaboration instead of to an inappropriate outworking of power.

It might be helpful, when reflecting on this conceptually, to split a SIAMS inspection into two main parts:

- Evidence-gathering
- Judgment-making

Evidence-gathering needs to be collaborative if it is to draw on the expertise of the right people at the right time, leading to comprehensive accuracy and understanding. The inspector needs the school to share their expert knowledge and understanding, so that they are able to understand the context and make sense of the evidence. This is the only way that the inspector can truly gain insight into the reality of the school, and they rely on the expertise of the school to enable them to do this effectively. Collaborative evidence-gathering occupies most of the time that is available during an inspection, so the establishment of good working relationships as quickly as possible is essential.

Once the evidence has been gathered, the collaborative aspect of the process is more or less over. It is at this point that the inspector retires to reflect and to make their *judgments*. This is *their* area of expertise and they conclude this aspect of inspection alone.

Successful, accurate and fair judgment-making is thereby reliant jointly on the effectiveness of the collaborative evidence-gathering process *and* on the subsequent application of the inspector's knowledge and expertise. A power-play is both unnecessary and unwarranted when carrying out inspection in a Christian manner.

Approachable Yet Firm

A caricature of a school inspector provides us with an immediate image of a suited and booted, po-faced, clipboard-wielding, unapproachable and largely disapproving individual. They do not smile, as to do so would compromise their superior professionalism and contingent power, and they ooze pomposity form every pore. 'The Trunchbull' (from Roald Dahl's *Matilda*) comes readily to mind as a person whom some think would make an excellent, albeit extreme and particularly mean, school inspector!

This unapproachable, rather terrifying individual is charged with putting members of a school community at their ease in order to gather all relevant evidence and apply it to the judgment-making process. At the very least, we can describe such an inspector as unapproachable, which begs the question of how members of a school community are meant to work with them, contributing meaningfully and evidentially to the judgments that are being made on the impact of the school's work.

Inspectors do not need to fear being approachable

Inspectors do not need to fear being approachable; it does not compromise their professional ability to be firm, to make judgments or to hold their ground in the face of challenge or disagreement. In fact, it is a tacit acknowledgment of the respective roles in together being part of the body of Christ in education—each with their own knowledge, skills and expertise; each playing their own part to the best of their ability. Approachability and firmness are not mutually exclusive qualities and both have a part to play in SIAMS inspection in a Christian manner.

Compassionate Yet Challenging

It is too easy to equate compassion with a lack of challenge, and thereby to assume falsely that, to be carried out in a Christian manner, a SIAMS inspection should simply give a school all that it could hope and wish for. But inspections do not always result in the outcomes that a school believes are warranted and, at times, school leaders are taken aback by the rigour with which a SIAMS inspector pursues evidence.

'It was more forensic than Ofsted,' comes the cry at times. Or, 'The inspector was far more challenging than we expected and we weren't prepared for that. That's not very Christian!'

This is one myth that definitely needs to be busted. To be characterized as Christian does not come with a contingent requirement to be lax, soft or vague. Each SIAMS inspector is charged—both legally and morally—with establishing a broad and robust evidence-base so that they can answer the Inspection Questions and reach a fair and accurate judgment. To do so means that they need to probe, challenge assumptions and, at times, push back when evidence is not forthcoming or does not appear to be supported by other findings. This may be contrary to what some might expect, especially if they have a false view of what is meant by 'in a Christian manner.'

Maybe as a result of outdated, pink-tinged, slightly blurred images of a gently-bearded Caucasian Christ smiling in a saintly manner at a small lamb or a compliant child, it is tempting to adopt an expectation that to be Christ-like, or Christian, means no more than to be indulgent. But this is not the example of the Christ whom we encounter in the New Testament. There, we meet a Christ who challenges that which he deems to be untruthful, unjust, discriminatory, unkind or corrupt. He dares to speak eternal truth to temporal power and he makes human the essential meaning of love. We are all familiar with the concept of 'tough love,' and we have probably meted it out at some point to those for whom we want the very best. Parents love their children too much to stand by and watch them act destructively. Teachers love their pupils too much to allow them to ignore boundaries or to sabotage their own success. And the church loves those who attend its schools too much to fail in its duty to highlight whether, through their vision and practice, the schools are living up to their foundation as church schools, thereby enabling pupils and adults to flourish.

Inspection in a Christian manner will always be respectful; it will always honour and dignify those involved; it will always be compassionate and take context into account; and it will always seek to understand the truth. Those carrying it out will always be cognisant of their status as fleeting guests within schools. They will be kind, open-minded, fair, expert and approachable, whilst simultaneously being determined, rigorous, challenging, authoritative and evidence-led.

Such is an inspection in a Christian manner.

7 Conclusion

In the 2023 Framework, SIAMS boldly embraces a radically different approach to school inspection in order to embed integrity at its heart. It does this by being explicit about the qualitative nature of the relevant evidence and, having asked high-level questions about impact, by making *judgments* on that evidence instead of awarding grades. In the process, it welcomes the stories of those in the community who are the experts in the life of the school, balancing this with the inspector's inspecting expertise. Crucially, it foregrounds each school's specific context, acknowledging that this can make all the difference in the world to the why, what and how of a school's Christian-vision-driven work. Thus, it is a radically different approach to school inspection.

However, being radically the same as that which recently preceded it, the 2023 SIAMS Framework does not reimagine what it means to be a church school. Certainly, it casts a spotlight on theologically-rooted Christian vision, but Christian vision has been a SIAMS expectation since at least 2018. With a focus on encouraging and enabling church schools to be the very best they can be for the benefit of the pupils and adults whom they serve, SIAMS quite simply asks *why* and *how* the school is the best church school it can be, and what this means for people's lives.

A good maxim for life, I find, is: 'The right thing is not always easy, but it is always right.' It is not easy to introduce such a radical change to the world of church school inspection and to forge a new path. However, research, the nature of SIAMS evidence, theologically-rooted Christian vision and the call to inspect in a Christian manner indicate that it is, in fact, the right thing to do.

Notes

1 Church of England Education Office, *Church of England Vision for Education: Deeply Christian, Serving the Common Good* (London: Archbishops' Council, 2016).

2 Education Act 2005 (London: Crown Copyright, 2005).

3 J Pritchard, *Education and the Church: Into the Next 200 Years* (London: General Synod of the Church of England, 2011).

4 H J Worsley, *What Motivates Christian Educational Practitioners? Theology as a School Resource* (Grove Education booklet eD17).

5 Education (Schools) Act 1992 (London: Crown Copyright, 1992).

6 Academies Act 2010 (London: Crown Copyright, 2010).

7 J Astley, 'Church Schools and the Church's Service for the Poor,' in H Worsley (ed), *Anglican Church School Education: Moving Beyond the First Two Hundred Years* (London: Bloomsbury, 2012) p 106.

8 The Statutory Inspection of Anglican and Methodist Schools, 'SIAMS Framework: September 2023' (2022). Available at: https://www.churchofengland.org/sites/default/files/2022-11/SIAMS%20Framework%20September%202023.pdf (accessed October 2022).

9 S J Ball, *Foucault, Power and Education* (Abingdon: Routledge, 2013) p 139.

10 M James, *In the Midst of Church School Inspection* (unpublished EdD thesis, Canterbury Christ Church University, 2018).

11 I F De Wolf and F J G Janssens, 'Effects and side effects of inspections and accountability in education: an overview of empirical studies,' *Oxford Review of Education*, 33:3 (2007), pp 379–396.

12 E Goffman, *The Presentation of Self in Everyday Life* (Edinburgh: University of Edinburgh, Social Sciences Research Centre, 1956).

13 M C M Ehren and A J Visscher, 'Towards a theory on the Impact of School Inspections,' *British Journal of Educational Studies*, 54:1 (2006) pp 51–72

14 C Thomas, *Implementing a vision for Christian education ethos: the experiences of school leaders and a sample of pupils in two schools* (unpublished PhD thesis, Canterbury Christ Church University, 2020).

15 J Astley and D Day (eds), *The Contours of Christian Education* (Southend: McCrimmons, 1992) pp 16, 21.

16 The National Society (Church of England and Church in Wales) for the Promotion of Education, 'SIAMS Report, St Mark's Church of England Junior School, Cheltenham,' 2022. Available at: https://primarysite-prod-sorted.s3.amazonaws.com/st-marks-ce-junior-school/UploadedDocument/214bf142-abf5-4cef-a56c-d6b1d4e0d7ad/siams-report-st-marks-church-of-england-junior-school-cheltenham-2022.pdf (accessed March 2023).